The Xenophobe's Guide to The Austrians

Louis James

RAVETTE PUBLISHING

Published by Ravette Publishing Limited
P.O. Box 296
Horsham
West Sussex RH13 8FH

Telephone: (01403) 711443
Fax: (01403) 711554

First printed 1994
Updated 1997
Reprinted 1998

Editor – Catriona Tulloch Scott
Series Editor – Anne Tauté

Cover – Jim Wire, Quantum
Printer – Cox & Wyman Ltd.
Production – Oval Projects Ltd.

Xenophobe's™ and
Xenophobe's Guides™
are Trademarks.

An Oval Project
for Ravette Publishing.

For providing the Austrian cakes on the
cover, grateful thanks are given to:

Gloriette Patisserie (Knightsbridge) Ltd.
128 Brompton Road,
London SW3

Contents

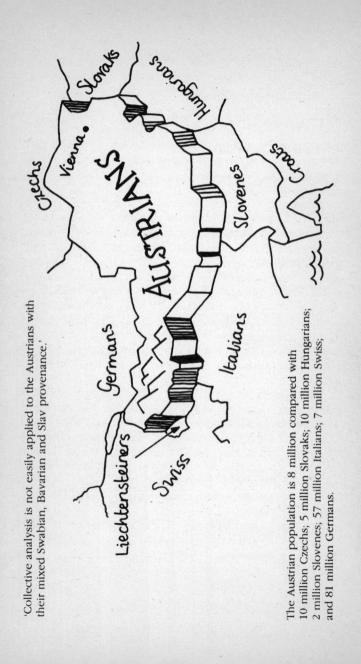

'Collective analysis is not easily applied to the Austrians with their mixed Swabian, Bavarian and Slav provenance.'

The Austrian population is 8 million compared with 10 million Czechs; 5 million Slovaks; 10 million Hungarians; 2 million Slovenes; 57 million Italians; 7 million Swiss; and 81 million Germans.

Nationalism and Identity

Forewarned

A great deal of ink has been spilt in Austria agonizing about Austrian identity. Does it actually exist? Should it exist? Is it expanding or diminishing? Is it drawn from the past only, or will it emerge in the future? Hypochondriacs worry about their ailments. Austrians worry about their identity.

Austrian identity is suspended somewhere between imperial history and parochial loyalties. 'In other countries,' writes an English historian, 'dynasties are episodes in the history of the people; in the Habsburg Empire, peoples are a complication in the history of the dynasty.' The Federal Republic of Austria only came into being in 1918 after the individual nations of the Habsburg's Austro-Hungarian Empire became independent; as Clemenceau rather brusquely put it: "*L'Autriche, c'est ce qui reste,*" i.e. Austria consists of what is left over.

Since the 19th century, Central Europe, the Balkans and now Russia have seen new states appearing like mushrooms after rain. While others came to the surface, Austria has stood out as a nation slowly submerging. A 94-year-old Austrian will have witnessed the demise of the Habsburg Monarchy, of the First Republic, of the Ständestaat (the clerico-fascist dictatorship), of the 'Ostmark' (the name applied to Austria by the Nazis), and of the four-powers occupation. Even Austria's joining of the European Union is seen by pessimists – much revered in Austria – as the beginning of the end for their Second Republic.

Non-Austrians, however, might be tempted to view such a history from the perspective of perverse optimism, for every ending has provoked a new beginning.

How Others See Them

A German historian once remarked a trifle ungraciously that Bavarians were the missing link between Austrians and human beings. He obviously forgot that the ancient Austrians actually came from Bavaria, give or take a few Alemanni.

The German view of Austrians has not mellowed with the passing of time. Hordes of Germans certainly come to beautiful Austria for skiing, hiking and sex; indeed, the German Chancellor spends his summer vacation at the Austrian lakes, trying unsuccessfully to lose weight. Unfortunately, this tends to reinforce the image of Austria as a place where you go when you are not being entirely serious, and of the Austrians as a not entirely serious people.

Germans feel the Austrians, especially the Viennese, have a tendency to *Schlamperei* (sloppiness or muddle), which the locals do not seem to view as a failing. ('The municipal vice of Vienna,' writes a more tolerant Englishman, 'is a sort of laziness, an easy-going spirit which quickly degenerates into slackness. It is shared by the highest and the lowest, causing the former to lose battles, the latter to forget errands.')

The German view of Austrian incompetence is no doubt rooted in history, for the Habsburg armies lost battles to the Prussians with monotonous regularity. The greatest catastrophe was Königgrätz (Sadowa, 1866), when Austrian soldiers rendered every possible assistance to the opposition's artillery by sporting decorative white uniforms, and the Austrian generals could not comprehend why the enemy consistently refused to adhere to the battleplan which they had patiently worked out in elegant manœuvres at home. As one commander plaintively remarked after the defeat: 'I cannot understand it. It always worked so well on the *Schmelz* (the parade ground in Vienna).' Germans are mystified by the Austrians' delight in telling this story against themselves. To a Prussian, self-irony about military defeats is a self-indulgence only too likely to lead to more of them.

Another German observation concerns the legendary (and largely mythical) Austrian meanness, the implication being that at least one nation is even more careful with money than are the Germans themselves. A Münchener gives a lift home to a Viennese. The Viennese does not offer to pay for petrol; what is more, he demands that they make an enormous detour to include the suburb of a town where he claims to have business. When they get there, it turns out he has twelve returnable bottles in the boot of the car. An advertisement in a Viennese paper had alerted him to the fact that a shop in this suburb pays five *Groschen* more for empties than anywhere else in Vienna. Seeing the look on the face of his German friend, he hastily offers to pay for the extra petrol. In the end he pays 300 *Schillings* to save 60 *Groschen*.

The Swiss are not unaware of latent Austrian animosity towards them and try to behave as tactfully as possible. While they cannot actually reduce the number of snow-capped mountains on their territory competing for skiers, they can at least ensure that a successful chain of Swiss-owned restaurants in Austria bears the name *Wienerwald* (Vienna Woods). When they swallow up Austrian enterprises, as they do from time to time, they adopt an avuncular manner, stressing their alertness to local sensibilities and portraying themselves as responsible partners generously pooling their expertise with Austrian colleagues.

However, not all Austrians are prepared to roll over and have their bellies scratched in this manner and rancorous attitudes persist. In a thin weekend for news, the story was splashed over the Austrian popular press that the roof of the Zürich public baths had fallen in, unfortunately with some loss of life. An elegant lady, reading about the tragedy in a Viennese cafe, was heard to murmur, "At last something has happened to the Swiss."

The Hungarians have learnt to regard their neighbours with some affection, particularly the proprietors of cut-price computer shops and used car lots. Budapestians live in daily expectation, or at least hope, of a wall of money from Austrian investors. Border villagers put up signs, with inscriptions in German, advertising hairdressers, dentists and more arcane wares.

The affection is, or was, reciprocal and the Viennese gave informal recognition to this economics-based love affair when they began referring to Mariahilferstrasse (Vienna's Oxford Street) as Magyarhilferstrasse. Unfortunately the Hungarians have now run out of cash and the Viennese are not terribly fond of penniless visitors. However, there are many Austro-Hungarian liaisons and the substantial areas of common ground between the two parties usually ensure that they are happy. An Austrian marrying into the controlled hysteria of a Hungarian family finds it is just like being at home, only more so, and a Hungarian finds that his Austrian in-laws cook mountains of heavy, calorie-rich food and force him to eat every scrap of it, just like his mother.

Austrians and Hungarians are not divided by a common language, as are Austrians and Germans, or English and Americans. The Hungarian therefore learns German, which for him is the language of money and career advancement, and charms everybody with his picturesque vowels and quaint Magyar idioms. None of his Austrian in-laws is so foolish as to attempt Hungarian which everyone knows is impossible, and he can thus continue to speak uninhibitedly on the family phone to his dodgy business friends in Budapest.

How They See Others

Austrians are deeply ambivalent about the Germans, undecided as to whether they should be portrayed as potential saviours or potential conquerors. It is impossible to ignore entirely the creeping Germanisation of the economy. (Large swathes of the popular press are 50% German-owned and almost any Austrian author who wants to make it into 'the big time' hastens to find a German publisher.)

Sometimes the Germans have to be humoured and honoured because they offer a kind of solution. For example, university professorships are frequently offered to German scholars, because internal politicking may have blocked all the viable local candidates. The acrimonious process of finding a new professor for the Chair of Modern History in Vienna could only be resolved by offering the post to a West German historian. To the dismay of all concerned, the intended recipient of this honour turned it down because the salary was too small. Austrian frustration is compounded by the fact that one part of the Austrian psyche is ready to assume a German scholar carries more weight than an Austrian, while another part of it thinks of the Germans as *Piefkes* (an abusive term which implies the humourless arrogance of the militaristic Prussian).

A major factor in Austrian economic stability and success has been the long-established policy of tying the Austrian *Schilling* to the *Deutschmark*. However, Austrian financial and journalistic circles affectionately refer to their currency as the 'Alpine Dollar' – not the 'Alpine Mark' which it really is.

The affinity, or lack of it, that exists between the Austrians and the Swiss is a compound of admiration, envy and contempt. Of course, a lot of people feel that way about the Swiss; but the Austrians have a particular difficulty in concealing their irritation with their neighbours for staying out of trouble and getting insufferably rich – even richer than the Austrians.

The Austrian's other neighbours are Italians, Slavs and Hungarians. With the Italians they would have been able to get along all right had the former not stolen South Tyrol in a shabby deal made with the allies during World War I. That can be overlooked, however, in view of the fact that Italians have traditionally supplied Austria with composers, architects, actors and ice-cream, all of which are popular. They also supply busloads of tourists. The Viennese shop assistants (who learn useful languages) are past masters at gently assisting linguistically incompetent Italian ladies to choose the most expensive items on offer.

The situation with the Slavs is more complicated. The Czechs were justifiably annoyed when Emperor Franz-Josef made a deal with the Hungarians in 1867, creating the Austro-Hungarian Empire. They failed to see why they did not qualify for the same treatment. (Answer: once you start on the Slavs, who knows where it will end?) Czechs supplied most of the construction workers in 19th century Vienna and gave the city such words as *tschechern* meaning to drink (alcohol of course) and *Tschecherl* which is a small coffee-house. Many would say that the Czechs have supplied the Austrian cuisine with its best item – dumplings. The entirely inoffensive Emperor Ferdinand, who was thought to be a button short, and was sent away to Prague, reportedly made one remark that gave the lie to his simple-mindedness, namely, "I am the Emperor and I shall have dumplings."

The Austrians' other Slav neighbours are the Slovenes and the Slovaks, who deserve a mention, which is all they usually get.

How They See Themselves

Austria is divided into nine *Länder* (Federal Provinces) which all see themselves as 'Austrian', especially when claiming their share of the Federal Budget. On the other hand they are defiantly Carinthian, Burgenlandian or Styrian (for example, when asked to help out with the nationwide distribution of asylum seekers or refugees). True, the inhabitants of Salzburg once expressed an overwhelming desire to become part of Germany and Vorarlberg attempted to slide off into Switzerland; but now everyone has decided to settle down and be Austrian. Or at any rate not something else.

Mere geographical complexities, however, are as nothing compared to the psychological complexities of Austrians as individuals. A Protestant from Tyrol may well exist in a parallel historical reality to a deeply Catholic Lower Austrian, while a second generation Viennese of Slavic origin has nothing in common with a Carinthian of German stock still dreaming of 'Greater Germany'.

When the celebrated Stone Age Austrian (nicknamed Ôtzi) popped out of a glacier in Tyrol in 1991, he was claimed by the Italians as one of them. A learned commission established that maybe he was lying just over the border by a metre or two, and a television reporter inquired satirically why they didn't "just look at his passport". The moral of this is: even the ice-man after all those years in cold storage is still as confused about his identity as all other Austrians.

Character

Collective analysis is not easily applied to the Austrians with their mixed Swabian, Bavarian and Slav provenance. As for the Viennese, the complexity of their miscegenation and the resulting contradictions in their character is legendary. Some say they are pleasure-loving, genial and possessed of a 'golden Viennese heart', while others regard them as devious, morose, time-serving and ill-natured. They can, in fact, be all of these.

The inhabitants of the other provinces seem more homogeneous, exhibiting characteristics determined in part by their situation and/or racial origin. In the Vorarlberger and the Tyrolese, for instance, one can recognise Swiss-type qualities of diligence, thrift, piety and stubbornness. Local patriotism is also intensely strong amongst the hot-blooded Carinthians in the south, whose notorious chauvinism is not unconnected with the presence of a sizeable Slovene minority.

As a result of the languages and intelligence of several peoples being gathered into a unity, the Austrians live in several diverse traditions and are thus capable of taking up different positions simultaneously. (It was an Austrian who set up the first Institute for the Study of Conflict and another, Richard Coudenhove-Kalergi, who first articulated the quaint idea of a Pan-European Union achieved by consent, not force.)

Other traits of the Austrian character that overleap provincial borders date back to the Metternich era (1814-1848) when conformity was imposed upon the whole population with an iron fist. Conformity on the one hand and a strategy of 'inner emigration' on the other became the traditional survival techniques adopted by Austrians when faced with *force majeure*.

Inner Emigration

Avoiding unpleasantness with the authorities has encouraged the dominance of presentation over substance. By the same token, the Austrians have two existences, one for the bureaucratic files and one for actual use. They have become past masters of parallel realities.

One consequence is that the Austrian character acquires a veneer beneath which frustration and resentment can grow like cancer, and here lies the root of the Austrian's ambivalent attitude to power, the mixture of obsequiousness and rancid contempt with which he approaches all that to him appear high and mighty. In Austria detonating pretension is a national pastime, one that can be enjoyed by all for the simple reason that the pretensions are there to be detonated. The playwright Franz Grillparzer who was in many ways the Austrian par excellence, a grumpy genius with a safe job in the state sector, remarked that his fellow-countrymen "held greatness to be dangerous and fame an empty vanity".

This opinion seems to have been ingrained in Austrians even before the collapse of their great empire. It has to do with attitudes to power that date back to an absolutist form of government and with the self-irony developed by people who were (or thought they were) more talented than the authority to which they had to defer. It has made the Austrians a fascinating mixture of the predictable and unpredictable, by turns kindly and malicious, steadfast and devious, over-confident and under-confident. It has made Austria a place where saloon-bar arrogance suddenly evaporates into spiritual humility and an over-developed sense of the ridiculous threatens genuine achievement and charlatanism alike.

It behoves the outsider to tread carefully in this hall of mirrors, where all generalisations are as true as their opposites. As TV weatherman Carl Michael Belcredi warned: "The multifariousness of the Austrians is similar to that of the weather with its infinite variety. That is why it's so difficult to do the weather forecast in this country. Everyone reckons they know better than the forecaster." The trouble is, they usually do.

Creativity versus Conservatism

The paradoxical character of the Austrian mingles profoundly conservative attitudes with a flair for innovation and invention. This creative tension usually takes the form of official obstructionism to good ideas, but sometimes the other way round. For example, the population were outraged by Josef II's attempt to make them adopt reusable coffins with flaps on the underside for dropping out the corpses. (The Emperor was forced to retreat, grumbling as he did so about the people's wasteful attitude.)

Rigid conservatism is blamed for what is gleefully described as the *österreichische Erfinderschicksal* – the supposedly typical Austrian fate of being ignored if you come up with a new invention. The powers-that-be, or their bureaucratic subordinates, are said to ward off unwelcome innovation using one of three possible lines of defence: '*Das hamma noch nie gemacht*' – 'We've never done that' (and we're not about to start); '*Das hamma immer schon so gemacht*' – 'We've always done it that way' (and are not about to change); or '*Da könnt' ein jeder kommen*' – 'Then anyone could come along' (and tell us to implement some footling idea like yours).

The Austrian needs lots of persuading to have his traditions tampered with in the name of modernisation and efficiency. He is attached to the religious holidays

14

that bespatter the calendar, highly anachronistic in a world where workers get generous holiday allowances. He is attached also to his sausage, his insipid beer, and the young white wine that tastes so remarkably like iron filings. He prefers the familiar, tried and tested to the novelty, the latter almost certainly being an attempt by persons unknown to make money at his expense.

Then again, he can equally well be open to new ideas and correspondingly impatient with the cant pumped out on behalf of vested interests and indolent reaction.

Janus-headed, the nation often seems to be looking backward even as it moves forward, and vice versa. Its hallmark is maintaining a certain ironic distance from the dead hand of the past and the claims of the future, such scepticism being appropriate to the inquiring Austrian mind. Thus one half is work mad, and the other half is all too aware of the vanity of human endeavour.

"Why are all these people running like hell?" goes a local joke. "They're competing in a marathon," comes the answer. "But why are they competing?" "Because the one who comes first gets a big prize.' "OK. But why are all the others competing?"

Attitudes and Values

A people that has been on the losing side in two world wars, endured a civil war, hyper-inflation and several spectacular stock-market crashes, all within the last three generations, may be forgiven for exhibiting a certain caution in its modus operandi. This may help to explain why Austrians have become the world's most fanatical savers, accumulating billions of *Schillings* in accounts

15

which often pay pitiful rates of interest.

Much treasured is the 'anonymous' *Sparbuch* (savings book), any attempt to abolish which is greeted with wailing and gnashing of teeth. Although the interest is taxed at source and therefore the gain from interest undeclared on the tax return tends to be minimal, the *Sparbuch*'s anonymity is a potent symbol of the little man's ability to cock a snook at authority – and of his determination to steer clear of risk. Leaving this sacred cow unslaughtered pleases everybody: the account holders who congratulate themselves on their business acumen, the Revenue which collects 25% tax from the interest, and the banks, whose laziness and greed are thus rewarded with a steady flow of cheap funds.

Status

The Austrian's quest for stability takes the form of a nostalgia for hierarchies that once determined man's place from the highest to the lowest rung on the social ladder. Until the removal of the Habsburg dynasty in 1918, the court remained the fount of all patronage. To get on in life you needed *Protektion*, i.e. a person who would recommend you for advancement. This is the origin of the Austrian obsession with titles and forms of address, which perform the twin functions of boosting your status in the eyes of those around you and of flattering the person who (you hope) will advance your interests.

Although all noble titles have long been banned by law, there is a seemingly unending list of professional titles to choose from. The most engagingly baroque handles are to be found in the Civil Service with titles like *Hofrat* (Aulic Councillor – the Aulic Council was founded in 1498). Of 19 titles listed in the Civil Service Directory of 1910, no less than 15 are still in use today.

Formal address, by title rather than by name, stretches downwards as well as upwards in Austria. It is claimed that government chauffeurs can attain the dizzy rank of *Fahrmeister* (driving master), provided they survive a few years in the job without any spectacular crashes.

As with bureaucrats, so with academics, whose various grades of achievement are punctiliously observed: even if you can only struggle by with a bachelor's degree, you can still style yourself on your nameplate as *Herr* or *Frau Magister* Schmidt, or, in the case of qualified engineers, as the impressive-sounding *Diplom-Ingenieur* Jones.

A Ph.D. brings the coveted title of *Doktor* (which can make all the difference when you are trying to get a table at a restaurant which is already over-booked). Should you reach the status of *Dozent* (university lecturer), you could then aspire to a Professorship, but this will only be 'Extraordinarius' (Associate) unless you manage to bag a Chair. The latter position is of such eminence that hall porters (the most acute barometers of social standing in Austria) project waves of sycophancy at your person as you pass, and a faint but detectable halo glimmers above your head when you deign to address the nation from a television studio.

Women professors are a rare species, so do not be fooled by the courtesy title '*Frau Professor*' which is acquired by the wives of professors through a process of social osmosis. The osmosis does not work the other way round, however, for in the male chauvinist world of Austrian academe there is no way the socially crushed husband of a *Frau Professorin* could get away with styling himself *Herr Professor*.

It is possible to by-pass the snakes and ladders of professional (and social) advancement by going into business and getting rich. When you have made it, you demonstrate the fact by building a villa in a favoured area for an astronomic sum (this was the undoing of the former Vice-Chancellor, Hannes Androsch, whose ostentatious villa provoked the Revenue to inquire into the source of his funds). If the villa is not considered prestigious enough on its own, you can always buy an Honorary Consulship for some obscure African country to go with it. As the citizens of such a country are rarely sighted in Austria, the work is not taxing but the representation looks good on your notepaper.

An important status symbol is the motor car – in particular Mercedes, Audis and BMWs. Even families with limited means usually buy the most prestigious car they can possibly afford, while *Gastarbeiter* traditionally invest in the larger Mercedes models, second-hand (sometimes very second-hand), for roaring back and forth between their homelands and Vienna, always with a full complement of family and most of the family assets.

All Austrians are experts on car prices which range from the grotesquely expensive to the obscenely over-priced. For this reason possession of the appropriate German model is a statement of net worth readily comprehensible to inferior beings such as Lada drivers and pedestrians.

Wealth and Success

The attitude of the average Austrian to money and success is at best ambivalent. Envy has something to do with this, but there is also a deep-rooted scepticism (based on what the man on the Vienna tram fancies he knows about the workings of the system). If somebody swims into the limelight, the first question everyone asks is: 'Who is behind him?' Of course he may have got where he has through talent and energy; on the other hand, as all properly informed persons will hasten to tell you, there are dozens of others equally or better qualified for the job.

There is a great deal of truth in this view. Austria is a small country with a generally highly educated population and it is unlikely that there will ever be enough top jobs to mop up all the able people. 'Who you know' is inevitably just as important as 'What you know'. Thwarted ambition is thus a chronic condition for a substantial and vocal sector of the population.

Relative paucity of opportunity and the continual necessity to guard one's rear have in the past led to a 'winner takes all' tendency in public life which increases the cynicism of ordinary mortals. There is even a phrase for it, *Ämterkumulierung* (job accumulation, a euphemism in most cases for 'salary accumulation'). When political muck-raking exposed the National Bank for having doubled as a honey pot for politically correct appointees, it transpired that the Governor received a salary which made that of the Head of the Federal Reserve in New York look like pin-money. More than one director was receiving princely remuneration for no visible contribution to the deliberations of the bank, and those who were asked to clear their desks in the wake of the furore may have had difficulty remembering where their desks actually were.

Religion

In Austria, as in other Catholic countries, piety co-exists with wealth in a manner calculated to do minimal injury to the image of either.

Citizens are reminded of their obligations to the church by the existence of a church tax; this is levied on the old English trade union principle that you pay it automatically unless you take the (considerable) trouble to opt out. Panic has recently broken out in the senior echelons of the church as the Association of Taxpayers has begun questioning the desirability, and even the ethics, of such a system. Bishops appear on television to explain the good work the church does in the field of charitable provision and of *Denkmalpflege* (preservation of monuments). Their entirely truthful protestations cannot quite conceal the root of the problem, namely the rising unpopularity of an institution that takes it upon itself to bully its flock about contraception and abortion, but expects people to forget that not very long ago it was all too ready to appease the Nazi regime.

The social and (to some extent) political control of the Austrian faithful by the Catholic Church reaches back to the Middle Ages, but it is now fighting a rearguard action against the erosion of its authority. It is precisely because the Austrians are devout and are anxious to give authority its due that the actions of blinkered ecclesiastics have such a disproportionately disruptive effect.

For centuries the faithful divided their abundant reserves of obedience between church and dynasty. Where their consciences compelled them to reject the official line, they adopted the tactic of 'inner emigration' – and thereby escaped from ideological conflict into happiness in a quiet corner of private life. But the existence of a dissident Catholic magazine, *Kirche Intern*, and the uncompromising attitude of the laity to reactionary bishops and to the recent sex scandal involving the former Cardinal Archbishop of Vienna, suggest that these days even the Austrians have had enough.

Behaviour

The Domestic Idyll

Home life for the Austrians is a never-ending quest for *Gemütlichkeit* or cosiness, which is achieved by accumulating objects that run the gamut from the pleasingly aesthetic to the mind-blowingly kitsch. The clutter is often sunk in a Stygian gloom, considered soothing and dignified by the proprietors, but which may make it difficult for a guest to locate his host, or to see what he is eating. While this is typical of old-style, middle-class living, modern apartments tend to veer towards the other extreme, exuding a brittle cheerfulness enhanced by pastel colours and stripped pine furniture from IKEA.

The average Austrian housewife is house-proud to the point of obsession. Slippers are provided so that visitors do not dirty the carpets which have been hoovered into a state of abject submission. Dust is conspicuous by its absence and WCs and baths gleam smugly as in advertisements for household cleansers. Children are permitted a certain amount of disorder in their rooms, but otherwise tidiness rules: pots, pans, glasses, tools, books, etc., have a primary function, that of being in their right place, which often seems to overwhelm their secondary function, that of being taken down and used.

Ideally, perfect harmony is achieved between *Ordnung* (order) and *Gemütlichheit*: in such a world no-one drops ash on the carpet and the lavatory paper never runs out. Mr. and Mrs. Österreicher perch happily in this never-to-be-fouled nest, making love and rearing their chicks in the time left over from cleaning and polishing.

Children

Austrian attitudes to children, as to so much else, appear to be contradictory. If the Austrian psychiatrist Erwin Ringel is to be believed, many children are permanently damaged by authoritarian attitudes, prudery about sexual matters and other parent-inspired ills.

Anyone with first-hand experience of an Austrian family and its demanding offspring will have difficulty believing this, for authoritarianism has largely given way to liberal attitudes. In fact, Austrian parents spend more money per capita per child per annum on toys than parents in any other European nation. As no-one has yet suggested that most of these toys are really for parental consumption, one must assume that children are the residual beneficiaries.

The Elderly

Austrian senior citizens may glare at rowdy children on trams and buses, but they are also capable of subjecting babies to uncritical admiration of the sort that would look excessive coming from the Madonna herself. (This could be said merely to demonstrate the older generation's preference for the *unmündig* over the *mündig*, i.e. for those who can't answer back over those who can.) Whether it is the final pay-off for the toy glut, or because of deeply ingrained social codes, Austrians tend to look after the aged and are less inclined to shove them off into homes as happens in Anglo-Saxon cultures.

But having a resident *Besserwisser* (know-all) discoursing easily and well on the right and the wrong way to bring up children inevitably leads to a certain amount of friction in the home. Since Austrian men dare not oppose their mothers openly, their wives are usually left to face this battle of wills alone. Social taboos will usually ensure suppression of rage in the domestic sphere, but persons in public life who have outstayed their welcome enjoy no such immunity: terms of abuse include *alter Trottel*, old moron, and the picturesque *Grufti*, one who has escaped from the tomb.

Animals

If you don't keep a grandmother in Austria, you may well keep a dog or a cat. Canine pets have reached such numbers in Vienna that 15 tons of fæcal matter are deposited monthly on the city streets.

To get to grips with the problem, a Parisian firm was summoned to Vienna to demonstrate its hit squad of orange-suited, motorised shit collectors going about their business. The mayor himself accompanied them as they flashed round the town vacuuming dog messes. However, it was quickly sensed that Viennese burghers would not take kindly to being terrorised on the pavements by whirlwind Dirty Fido operatives. A democratic solution to dog shit has yet to be found.

A special place in Austrian affections is reserved for the horse; not that many people can afford to keep one, but horses have traditionally been seen to lend extra dignity to humans, especially emperors and generals. The most famous Austrian horses are, of course, the Lipizzaners, who perform a ballet-like dressage in the Spanish Riding School of Vienna's Hofburg. These beautiful white beasts enjoy all the cosseting befitting an Austrian state employee, i.e. generous holidays and an Indian summer of handsomely-pensioned tranquillity. As one of the country's biggest foreign currency earners their cachet is rivalled only by that of the Vienna Philharmonic and the Vienna Boys' Choir. Lipizzaners would seem to have realised every man's dream of achieving social prestige combined with job security. No wonder that all little Austrian boys, as the saying goes, 'want to be members of the Vienna Boys' Choir in their youth and, thereafter, a Lipizzaner stallion'.

Immigrants

The Austrians' Southern Slav neighbours are encountered mainly in the shape of *Gastarbeiter* (guest workers), who are concentrated in Vienna, where they are employed in the construction and service industries. 10% of the population of Vienna are foreigners, of which nearly half come from former Yugoslavia. Many have been working and paying taxes in Austria for years and the Employers' Federation is among their stoutest supporters.

Some anti-foreigner feeling can be heard in bars, where there are mutterings about the *Tschuschen* (an insulting term for Balkan peoples) who are a familiar sight at the Südbahnhof (the railway station for the south) with their *Tschuschen-Koffer* (*Tschuschen* suitcases, i.e. plastic bags). All the same, the Austrians acknowledge that these industrious people do the dirty jobs that they themselves have become too grand to do.

Although there are some problems with schools that are flooded with immigrant children, the age-old Viennese absorption mechanism is at work – through Austrian education Slav children become bilingual and are then indistinguishable from their counterparts in history who underwent the same process – and whose names fill the Viennese telephone book. (As early as 1787 it was stated that no Viennese family 'could trace its indigenousness further back than three generations'.)

The cabaret artist Hugo Wiener illustrates this assimilation process in a sketch which is set in an office of the Aliens Bureau where two officials are interviewing a Turk for extension of his residence permit. With elaborate pantomime and pidgin German they convey various questions: Is he married? Does he work? Where does he live? A sympathetic member of the public even tries to assist in the communication process, but is told by an official to mind his own business. It is clear the Turk has difficulty in understanding the frequently misleading pantomime, and the questions with their broken syntax.

At length another official arrives, and unaware of what has been going on, asks the Turk the same questions very rapidly in Viennese dialect. To the astonishment of the first two officials the Turk answers equally rapidly and at considerable length in faultless German. "Gracious!" exclaims one of the officials, "And there we were trying to make things easy for him by explaining everything in Turkish."

Queuing

It is well known that the ability or inability to queue marks the difference between the 'European' and the 'Balkan' mentality. That the Balkans lie on the doorstep may be deduced from the Austrians' way of queuing, the art of which they have nearly mastered, but not quite.

The average Austrian does stand in line, demonstrating his European side, but his preference is to edge forward until he is level-pegging with the person in front. He always seems to be on the point of barging the queue, but never actually does. Apart from inducing a state of nervous agitation in the person ahead of him, this is a relatively harmless manoeuvre, except in banks. Here the cashiers have felt obliged to paint two yellow footprints a couple of metres short of the teller's window and to display a notice which states that, in the interests of client confidentiality, no-one should overstep the footprints until it is their turn to be called. Since all Austrians are obsessed with their anonymous accounts, this is a message even compulsive queue-edgers can take on board.

Driving

In one area of activity Balkan habits prevail, namely driving. The unbridled aggression of the average Austrian driver may partly be due to the frustrating road conditions in his small country, but it also seems to be a character trait. If you obey the speed limit, you will soon have a purple-faced Opel ogre on your back bumper, flashing his lights. If you signal to filter across the lines on a ring road, as likely as not a Mercedes mugger accelerates from behind to block your passage. The principal tactics of the Viennese road-hog are cutting in while pretending that his victim is the one failing to observe lane discipline, horn-blowing as soon as the lights turn to green, and light-flashing at all and sundry.

A gentleman who has just taken leave of you with a show of elaborate and flowery courtesy may fail to recognise you from his car only moments later as you cross a dark street, and is quite capable of driving full tilt at you, while mouthing abuse through the window.

As soon as he gets behind the steering wheel, the

Austrian male is transformed from mouse to monster. The unruffled businessman, the mild and courteous burgher, even the fawning waiter is suddenly a caveman on wheels. The highway is where the Austrian feels he has a licence to blow off steam and show the world that, however much he may be humiliated and pushed about at the workplace or hen-pecked at home, there is still a little corner of his soul that is for ever Arnold Schwarzenegger.

Manners

Greetings and Forms of Address

Austrians are sticklers for formal manners. Hand-shaking is a national pastime and latecomers to committee meetings hold up proceedings until all available flesh has been pressed; and woe betide anyone who fails to greet, whether entering a shop or buying a postage stamp.

The usual Austrian greeting is the South German *Grüss Gott*, but the socialist-inclined, who are careful to leave God out of the matter, greet with *Guten Tag*. There are flattering forms of address which can be employed either ironically, or as a perfectly genuine display of courtesy. An ascending scale of deferential verbal approaches ranges from *Meine Hochachtung* ('My deep respect' – unpleasant letters from the bank always end with *hochachtungsvoll* – with deep respect), through *Meine Verehrung* (My reverence) to *Meine Ergebenheit* (My devotion). From time to time one receives letters that close with an expression of regard to one's 'revered wife' (*verehrte Gattin*) and sign off with a verbal flourish such as *Ihr ergebener...* (Your devoted...).

These formulas have their origin in the etiquette books of the early 19th century and in the nuances of the social pecking order under the Austro-Hungarian Empire. An elderly lady who was born when the Empire still had several years to run, prefaces the name on the envelopes of her letters with the style *Wohlgeboren* (well-born). Increasingly archaic, though still heard, is the chivalrous approach to women with the words *Küss die Hand* (I kiss your hand), but it is not always well received if you actually proceed to do so. A sideways motion of the bowed head a few centimetres above the hand in question is considered more than adequate and avoids the humiliation of having it abruptly withdrawn just before labial impact.

Other somewhat outmoded forms of address have also entered the province of irony, largely due to their merciless exploitation by cabaret artists and the tidal waves of feigned deference emanating from Viennese waiters, e.g: *Gnädiger Herr* – Your Lordship, *Habedieehre* – May I have the honour, and *Gschamsterdiener* – Your most obedient servant. *Gnädige Frau* – Gracious Lady or Madam, can be either ironic or sincere according to context, so watch out.

Young people and intimates dispense with formal greetings and leave-takings, contenting themselves with *Servus*, *Grüss Dich* and (in Vienna) *Papa*. This informality should not lead one to suppose that the act of greeting has become any the less important. Not to greet is regarded as a personal affront and there are few greater solecisms that an Austrian can commit. When Karl Kraus wrote a hostile obituary of the Archduke Franz-Ferdinand after the latter's assassination in 1914, his most damning indictment of the man who indirectly caused the first World War was the accusation: *Er war kein Grüsser* ... ('He didn't greet ...').

Invitation to Dinner

The prelude to an Austrian dinner is often a glass of fruit *Schnaps*, which should be tipped down the throat in a single motion. As this is drunk on an empty stomach, it has an effect roughly equivalent to throwing paraffin on the living-room fire and is considered a satisfactory method of kick-starting the evening's entertainment. Austrians are used to these preliminaries and show no reaction beyond a slightly enhanced glitter of the eyeballs.

Another important point of drinking etiquette arises once you are seated at the table. Nobody is allowed to drink until the host has raised his glass and toasted the company *Prost, Zum Wohl*. Lashing into the wine without waiting for this ritual will attract incredulous looks, even if, as sometimes happens, the host is so busy holding forth that he has forgotten to fire the starting-gun. An absent-minded sip may attract the softly-spoken comment: 'Are we drinking English-style tonight?' which at least reminds the host of his duties, but does nothing for the amour-propre of the guilty party.

The green light for eating usually takes the form of a similar verbal ritual – *Guten Appetit, Mahlzeit* – but after that you're on your own, literally so in the case of many foreigners, for Austrians are used to heavy food and can despatch astonishing quantities of it very rapidly and in a manner that might be said to display grace under pressure.

Even outside the realm of social eating and drinking Austrian manners remain disciplined and orderly. Formality is cultivated, and admission into a relationship of intimacy, i.e. the switch from *Sie*, the formal 'you', to *Du*, the informal one, can only be initiated by the elder of the people concerned. (When the magic moment comes, he may raise his glass to you and pronounce his Christian name; you respond in kind and thereafter need have no further worry about revealing your tax evasion scheme in his presence.)

A woman is more likely to announce: "We are now on *Du* terms" (it is her prerogative), while the younger generation have mostly shortened the incubation period for the birth of a *Du* relationship to a few meetings, or even a few hours. In environments that constitute a sort of *de facto* freemasonry, such as the students' canteen in the university, there is a tendency to dispense with *Sie* altogether. On the other hand, colleagues who have spent a lifetime working at neighbouring desks may adhere ostentatiously to the *Sie* form, especially if they hate each other.

Leisure and Pleasure

Mountain Walking and Hiking

Walking in the Alps and hiking in the Vienna Woods are (or originally were) middle-class activities, often conducted with a Pooterish earnestness and dignity that brings to mind F.W. and E. Möller's 1954 worldwide hit, 'The Happy Wanderer', in particular the immortal lines: 'I raise my hat to all I meet, And they raise back to me', followed by the cautious ecstasy of its refrain: 'Fal de rih, fal de rah, fal de ra ha ha ha, ra ha ha ha, rah!'.

As far as the Viennese are concerned, a good day's rambling in the dark and gloomy Wienerwald is just what the doctor ordered, and can be combined with the ritualistic activity of *Schwammerlsuchen*, mushroom hunting. In the late afternoon comes the climax of the day, a

Jause, euphemistically described as a 'snack', but to non-Austrians a full meal.

The uniform for all this activity is a symbol of the great outdoors, Austrian-style, namely Lederhosen (leather breeches) and a dark felt hat with a thing like a shaving brush stuck in the hat-band. You do not have to be a mountaineer to wear it. Walking through Vienna's 15th District visitors might be surprised to encounter a gentleman in full Alpine rig* hurrying along with a purposeful air. He is, in fact, setting out for an afternoon of sublime rusticity in his *Schrebergarten* or allotment.

Allotments

Named after Daniel Gottlob Schreber, the 19th century German founder of the Small Garden Movement, *Schrebergärten* do not, in fact, conform to the founder's original concept which envisaged playground-parks for young people. Instead they were first encouraged after World War I so that people could grow their own vegetables in a time of shortage. Later they became the summer retreats (in true Austrian style hedged around not only by greenery, but also by innumerable rules and regulations) for the inhabitants of dank tenement houses on modest incomes.

The *Schrebergärten* of today are the last word in *Gemütlichkeit*, each with a profusion of lovingly tended fruit trees and flowers, a pocket-handkerchief of lawn and a summer house. Many also boast a full complement of

---

*Unlike the happy wanderer, the urban hiker's hat sports a number of subtle differences of cut and presentation, for example, the addition of silly badges.

garden gnomes, indistinguishable in certain lights from their owners.

Spectator Sports

The most popular spectator sports are naturally those at which Austrians excel – winter sports and motor-racing. The former is to be expected but the latter is a bit of a puzzle. It is true that in the 19th century an Austrian developed one of the first internal combustion engines, like a number of other Austrian inventors receiving little recognition and less thanks for doing so; but Niki Lauda is a phenomenon that has inspired a whole generation of Formula I aspirants.

Austria's winter sportsmen, especially skiers, are in a class of their own. A newcomer to the country might think the Austrian sports commentators' endless recitation of their countrymen's names mere chauvinism, until he realises that in most competitions several of the first ten places will have been won by Austrians. As soon as some local hero has clipped a second off the slalom record or barely survived a death-defying ski-jump, a microphone is thrust in his face and he is invited to give his view of the matter. As this is usually delivered in impenetrable Tyrolean dialect, German-speakers are little the wiser; however the translation always turns out to be something like: "I didn't think I could do it; but then I jumped; and then I did it!"

The career of a top-class ski-racer being somewhat short-lived, it is important to collect as many titles and give as many television interviews as possible before retiring to open a hotel or to advertise washing powder.

Sex

The Austrians display for the most part a civilised and down-to-earth attitude to the physical side of affairs of the heart. Most quietly ignore the attitude of the Catholic church to such matters as contraception and abortion (the latter is legal in Austria if carried out in the first three months of pregnancy). Prudery is lacking in the Austrian temperament and chastity is regarded as something only suitable for those who have chosen it.

Austrians are more relaxed about irregular liaisons than more judgmental northerners. The euphemisms for describing the participants lack the prurience beloved of English puritans. A gallant who makes love to a married woman may be known as the *Hausfreund* (house friend) – an innuendo that often attaches to similar words such as *Freundin* (female friend); and unmarried people in steady relationships are each other's *Lebensgefährten* and *Lebensgefährtinnen*, terms which conjure up a pleasing image of companions on the long road of life.

An anecdote sums up the general attitude to irregular sexual arrangements. Two men meet for the first time at a party. By way of conversation one says to the other, "You see those two girls chatting to each other in the corner? The brunette is my wife and the pretty blonde she's talking to is my mistress." "That's funny," says the other man, "I was just about to say the same thing, only the other way round."

Obsessions

Apart from their relatively modern obsession with motor cars (one should not forget that Ferdinand Porsche and Niki Lauda are among Austria's most illustrious sons), Austrians have two enduring obsessions: collecting, and death.

Collecting

Collecting may be traced back to the Habsburgs, who accumulated new territories, titles and treasures as lesser men collect stamps.

Few Austrians can afford to collect as they did, but one contemporary collector, the oculist Rudolf Leopold, has accumulated such a store of priceless Klimts, Schieles and works by major Austrian painters that an entire building is to be reserved for it in a projected new museum complex and Leopold himself has been appointed director for life. (The story goes that his family once begged him to take a picture to Sotheby's in London in order to raise much-needed cash. Eventually he was persuaded, went to London, sold the picture and bought another with the proceeds.)

Happily for the ordinary Austrian there are lots of more affordable substitutes he can collect. Kitchen walls are plastered with folk pottery from surrounding countries and living rooms are filled with assiduously collected souvenirs from holidays abroad – a gondolier on a glass boat, three different sizes of cow-bell, or a donkey with a nodding head.

Even as austere a figure as Sigmund Freud pedantically collected 'antiquities' on his visits to Italy and Greece, later transferring them to London when he had to flee

Vienna. A recent exhibition of these harmless knick-knacks is furnished with a catalogue containing solemn exegesis of the relationship between Freud's ideas and his antiques.

The Austrian's obsession with small, charming and useless objects has made him a shrewd judge of which parts of the Austrian heritage can best be marketed, and the souvenir industry offers foreign tourists several lines of shameless kitsch, which include figurines of Franz-Josef (*Kaiser-kitsch*) chocolates known as *Mozartkugeln* (i.e. Mozart balls) and even Klimt or Schiele T-shirts. In this way the Disneyland version of Austria past and present makes Austrians rich and foreigners happy.

Death

The Austrians' fascination with death also owes something to aristocratic tone-setting, notably the obsequies that made the death of an emperor something to look forward to. The spectacular aspect of funerals – what the Viennese call a *schöne Leich* (lovely corpse) – plays a vital role in their culture. This is because the Austrians believe that death is a part of life, not simply the termination of it. 'He who would understand how a Viennese lives,' wrote Hermann Bahr, 'must know how he is buried; for his being is deeply bound up with his no-longer-being, about which he is constantly singing bitter-sweet songs.'

Rituals connected with death range from the picturesque to the macabre. In the former category is the custom whereby colleagues bearing the body of a former leading player at the Burgtheater make a circuit of honour of the theatre before the coffin is despatched to the cemetery. In the macabre category is the gruesome necrolatry of the Habsburgs. For hundreds of years deceased emperors were carved up and distributed around the capital: hearts were deposited in silver urns in the Church of the Augustinians, the embalmed entrails went into the catacombs of St. Stephen's and the rest of them landed up in the Capuchin crypt.

Death-oriented attractions in Vienna include the Burial Museum, in which the star item is a coffin with a bell-pull to alert passers-by should you happen to have been buried alive, and the vast Central Cemetery. The latter is a place of pilgrimage, especially on All Saints Day, when most of Vienna travels out through the November mists to place a wreath on a family tomb or on the *Ehrengrab* (grave of honour) of some favourite actor or public figure. The cemetery is so large that the municipality runs a minibus to ferry the elderly along its silent avenues and employs a sharp-shooter who ventures out at dawn to shoot hares breakfasting on the succulent wreaths.

Suicide

Death and disposal come to us all in time, but a remarkably large number of Austrian intellectuals decide to pre-empt the decision of the Almighty. Attempts to generalise about this penchant for self-destruction soon run into the obstacle that there seem to be as many causes as there are cases. Noteworthy, however, is the gay abandon with which strict Catholic prohibitions are jettisoned when Austrians decide enough is enough.

Some suicides seem eminently rational as responses to protracted and fatal illness (e.g. those of the writers Adalbert Stifter, Ferdinand von Saar and Ludwig Hevesi); others were apparently the result of miscalculation, like that of playwright Ferdinand Raimund, who erroneously

36

thought he had contracted rabies after a dog-bite. In a quite different category was the case of the philosopher and self-styled genius Otto Weininger, who committed an attention-seeking suicide in the house where Beethoven died, whereas the physicist Ludwig Boltzmann, who really was a genius, ended his life as a consequence of depression and overwork.

Professor Ringel's strictures on Austrian parents are lent some support by the long list of suicides among the offspring and siblings of the famous. It includes two of Wittgenstein's brothers, the sons of the physicist Ernst Mach and of the writer Hugo von Hofmannsthal, the daughter of Arthur Schnitzler and the brother of Gustav Mahler. There was also the architect Eduard van der Null who sank into terminal despair when the Emperor made a slighting remark about his opera house.

Another artist, Alfred Kubin, and the composers Alban Berg and Hugo Wolf all attempted suicide. Not to be outdone, the dynasty supplied the most spectacular suicide of all, when Crown Prince Rudolf shot his lover, Marie Vetsera, and then himself at Mayerling. Rudolf, who kept a skull on his desk as a memento mori, was simply one more in a long line of Austrians who opted for the short cut to the other side (although shooting his mistress at the same time was overstepping the conventions somewhat).

A bonus for an Austrian of being safely dead is that his removal from the scene often brings the applause and recognition that was denied him in life. Mortality is the pre-condition for immortality, or so it is often claimed, and Mozart is paraded as the 'awful example'. Mahler supplied a good aphorism to buttress the myth: *Muss man denn in Österreich erst tot sein damit sie einen leben lassen?'* – "Have you actually got to be dead in Austria before they'll let you live?"

Shopping

Austrian consumers have a great variety of goods to choose from at prices ranging from the expensive to the extremely expensive. This is partly because VAT is levied at a high rate, but there are other factors such as restrictive practices resting on archaic laws, and the operation of thinly-veiled cartels. Predictably, expectations of lower prices after entry into the EU have been dashed. The public has found Austrian businessmen to be infinitely resourceful in their rearguard action. Ailing Tyroleans are busily polishing their Italian, since medicines may be up to 40% cheaper over the border.

In supermarkets the model shopper gives an earnest of his intent to buy when he collects a wire basket or trolley at the entrance. All Austrians dutifully do this so that they cannot be accused of slipping things into their pockets as they go round. Approaching the checkout, customers are confronted by large notices stating that personal shopping bags should be held up for inspection 'to avoid misunderstandings'.

A further irritation to the humble shopper is the way the large food chains plaster the inside of their stores with placards telling the customers what a good deal they are getting. So far from this being the case, 1993 saw some big names exposed for a swindle of such stunning simplicity that one wonders why no-one had thought of it before: as soon as the expiry date on packaged meat had come round, the products were removed from the shelves, conscientiously restamped with a new expiry date and returned to display.

Much more congenial than the big stores are the little men of Austrian retailing – stall-holders, lottery ticket vendors, 'Tabak' proprietors who sell taxation stamps and tickets for public transport as well as newspapers and tobacco, and, last but not least, the *Greißler*. The latter are a Viennese phenomenon, corner-shop grocers who are said to be always on the verge of extinction due to supermarket competition (but who have been on the verge for at least 30 years). *Greißler* have been described as 'selling everything from gherkins to homespun philosophy'. The substantial amount of the latter being transacted means they are often full of pensioners chattering like starlings. The shrewd owners remain studiously neutral on the burning issues of the day to safeguard their customers' continued patronage. The Tabaks and lottery shops also attract their *Stammkunden* (regulars), who like to linger over a cigarette while offering their captive audience a beguiling mixture of provincial wit and wisdom. Whenever a public scandal hits the headlines, it is hardly possible to get in, so great is the press of persons wishing to air an opinion.

Traditionally, Austrian conservatism and union power jointly dictated that shopping hours accorded with the convenience of shop-keepers, rather than with that of their customers. After endless wrangles, opening times have been somewhat liberalised. Even so, a number of shops and services, such as sub-post offices and some bank branches, close for one or even two hours over lunchtime. Austrians are understanding about this; lunch, after all, is a serious matter, and making money should not be allowed to take precedence over the workings of the digestion.

One might think that the mere right to open your shop more or less when you saw fit should not be contentious, but people who think like this fail to understand the Austrian shop-keepers' mentality. If the shop-keeper doesn't himself want to open at a particular time, then of course he wants a law preventing anyone else from doing so.

Eating and Drinking

Although things are now changing, food habits in Austria have been dictated for a very long time by quantity rather than quality. The names for many traditional dishes are redolent of quivering mounds of food exploding on the palate like the cholesterol bombs they so often describe. *Bauernschmaus*, for instance, means 'peasants' treat' and consists of a great heap of meats and/or sausages only a little smaller than the Grossglockner*, garnished with dumplings and sauerkraut. Macho eaters can test their staying power on *Beuschel* (chopped offal in sauce) or *Blunzn* (black pudding).

We are what we eat, so perhaps it is inevitable that some middle-aged Austrians bear a striking resemblance to popular items on the national menu such as *Fleischknödeln* (potato dumplings filled with meat) and *Grammelknödeln* (more dumplings, only stuffed with pork scratchings). On the other hand, the Emperor Franz-Joseph remained lean until he died at a great age, perhaps because he ate the Viennese speciality of *Tafelspitz* (boiled beef) every single day. At a time when everyone from middle-ranking bureaucrats to commissionaires of apartment blocks expressed their patriotism by turning themselves into Franz-Josef look-alikes, the Emperor's eating habits had a powerful impact on the sales of boiled beef. It remains a favourite dish even today, although the purists' insistence on cooking it for four hours can result in gastronomic meltdown.

Boiled beef, however, has never achieved the universal approbation enjoyed by that other speciality, the *Wiener Schnitzel*. A decent *Wiener Schnitzel*, say the cognoscenti, should be 'the size of a lavatory seat' (*abortdeckelgross*)

*Austria's highest mountain.

and, just as with lavatory seats, it is frowned upon to share one between two. The real thing, dipped in egg and breadcrumbs, fried in butter until golden brown, and seasoned with lemon is, in itself, worth the journey to Vienna.

Cake, Bake and Take

Vienna shares with Salzburg (and indeed virtually any Austrian town worthy of the name) a *Konditorei* (cake shop) tradition that would fulfil Billy Bunter's wildest dreams.

All over Austria ladies of a certain age and girth gravitate in the mid-afternoon to the nearest cake shop. The choice before them is bewilderingly large – a dazzling range of cakes with the names of the chefs who invented them or the aristocrats who consumed them (Sacher, Esterhazy, Malakoff, Dobos); there are sponge slices garnished with blackberries, bilberries, raspberries or strawberries; not to mention the petits fours, chocolate fingers, and strawberry tarts. The *Konditorei* is primarily a female haunt, a place where ladies who have accepted defeat in the battle of the bulge can sink comfortably into late middle age like ships sliding slowly beneath the waves.

Bäckerei (bakeries) have an astonishing range of wheat or rye loaves, many of them seasoned with cumin. The latter is valuable as a carminative, which explains the intestinal winds approaching gale force that often follow the consumption of Austrian bread. Bakeries also offer brioches, croissants, filled rolls and numerous pastries. For those who want to devour their purchases on the spot with a cup of coffee, there is usually a counter along

41

the back wall. This facility is much used by the ubiquitous Viennese *Plaudertaschen* (gossipy windbags) airing a few scandals as they scoff their *Plundertaschen* – puff pastries filled with plum jam.

Urban Austrians appear to need gastronomic support even for the merest walk to the post office or the newspaper stand: how else can you account for the fact that every few yards you are assailed by good smells from a confectioner or bakery, a doughnut stand, a sandwich shop, a butcher's shop with its own *Stehbeisl* (eating counter) or a *Würstelstand*?

The latter are placed in strategic proximity to public transport junctions and offer a variety of hot sausages such as *Frankfurters*, fat-squirting *Debreziners* and *Burenwurst*. The gherkins, mustard and roll that accompany these delicacies represent a largely futile attempt to break down or mop up the fat content. The least enticing substance on offer from the *Würstelständ* is *Leberkäse* or meat-loaf which has a faintly disturbing pink complexion, turning slowly to grey when in terminal decline. It sits in its glass oven on the counter, sweating slightly and giving off a pungent odour, as if defying you to eat it.

The attractions of cheap food like this in a land of nightmare prices are obvious enough; and even if price were not a consideration, it is doubtful whether the real Austrian trencherman would be greatly impressed by food that might prolong life and keep the waistline in check. He prefers to contemplate, with admirable stoicism, the not entirely disagreeable prospect of *Selbstmord mit Messer und Gabel* ('suicide with a knife and fork').

Drinking

The Austrians' enthusiasm for indifferent beer is as nothing when compared to their passion for fizzy young wine. In wine growing areas the local inns are known as *Heurigen*. The name comes from the word *heuer* meaning 'this year', and indicates that only young wine from the previous harvest and from a single vineyard can be offered. Atmosphere and tradition are what distinguish the *Heurige*, being just as important as the quality of the (mostly white) wine, which many prefer to drink *gespritzt* (splashed with soda water).

The quality most associated with drinking is *Gemütlichkeit*, which in this context implies informality, conviviality and cosiness. Geniality usually takes a form that is bewildering to those not fully attuned to the vagaries of the Austrian character, for the thoughts of many, when in their cups, soon turn to depression and death. *Heurige* songs (sung in Viennese dialect) reflect this: "You can't say much, it's too bloody loud, And what could you say that's halfway fit? If you are all burned out and void, Company soothes you, at least a bit."

The undertow of melancholy, for which the wine is no doubt responsible in more ways than one, undercuts the unrestrained sentimentality and gives *Heurige* drinking sessions a macabre spice like a drop of urine in a cup of nectar. A modern troubadour, Roland Neuwirth, has satirized this tendency in his *Genuine Viennese Song* which offers 15 metaphors for dying. These include: 'to lower yourself', 'to lay aside your slippers', 'to hand in your spoon', 'to begin to view the potatoes from underneath', and 'to put on wooden pyjamas'.

Sense of Humour

The keynote of Austrian humour is self-depreciation, a dearly clung-to conviction that things turn out badly, even when they turn out well; this is the refined Austrian version of the famous Italian insight: 'We were better off when we were worse off.'

Austria's history is the soil that nurtured a humour of damage limitation or graceful resignation, one that pours the balm of self-mockery on the wounds of small and great defeats. The attitude was admirably summed up by an Austrian general, who reacted to the approach of yet another military catastrophe with the airy observation: "the situation is hopeless, but not serious".

The Austrian favours wit and irony, rather than the pun. Wit is employed to invent wonderfully vivid names, a skill developed to the highest degree by the comedian and playwright Nestroy, whose works are littered with creations such as *Lumpazivagabundus*, a word concocted from *Lump* (meaning a scoundrel) and vagabond.

Viennese dialect is particularly rich in vividly descriptive coinages such as *Grabennymphen* (Graben nymphs), a term for prostitutes dating from the time they thronged the Graben which is now the most fashionable street in Vienna. (It is said that Count Taaffe, the Prime Minister, on taking a post-prandial stroll there, noted with surprise the absence of the *Nymphen*. His companion, a municipal official, explained that they had been cleared into the back streets because their very great number made it "no longer possible to distinguish honest women from the tarts". "Maybe you and the police can't," said Taaffe drily, "but the rest of us manage it perfectly well.")

Viennese humour is variously distilled from the sly surrealism of the Czechs, the gallows wit and professional

44

pessimism of the Hungarians, and the Italian tradition of clowning and mimicry. Jewish writers and cabaret artists have also contributed their own brand of acerbic observation, the threatened underdog's traditional tactic for deflecting aggression.

Defensive wit is an enduring element in the Austrian's rueful view of the world and his own diminished place in it. Nostalgia may be milked for tourism, but Austrians have a more ambivalent view of their past, as many jokes underline. The comedian Karl Farkas has a sketch in which the ghost of Emperor Franz-Josef (who died in 1916) returns to earth for a chat with him. "Tell me, Farkas, how did the First World War turn out?" asks the Emperor, by way of conversation. "Unfortunately, not well, your Majesty," says Farkas. "That I didn't want," sighs the old man. "Me neither," agrees the comedian courteously.

Irony puts the great in their place, but also permeates the average Austrian's view of himself, which is much the same thing as his '*Weltanschauung*'. "The Austrian tends to navel-gazing," remarks a contemporary politician, "by which I mean he sees in himself the whole world." Such inverted provincialism is beautifully caught in Josef Hader's film *Indien*, which describes the life of two petty bureaucrats. When one of them is dying, his colleague visits him in hospital. Gazing at the night sky from the hospital balcony, they fall into philosophical reverie. "I want to know the answer to so many things," says the younger man; "for example, where does the rain come from?" "From the clouds," says his knowledgeable friend. "Ah, but where do the clouds come from, Herr Bösel? Tell me that!" "Mostly from Ireland, I think."

The Austrian's depiction of himself as a self-absorbed bit-player on the great stage of life constitutes a leitmotif of the nation's humorous self-perception. It is seen as much in Nestroy's famous claim: 'Success decides nothing', as it is in a contemporary graffito scrawled on the interior of a Viennese tram: 'Knowledge pursues me but I am faster!'

Yet the Austrian capacity for self-denigration has a harsh and bitter side, and even as the outsider begins to explore the possibility that all this persiflage conceals a darker truth, he finds the Austrian has got there first. "I expect the worst from everybody, including myself," said Nestroy, "and I am seldom disappointed."

Culture

Until the 20th century, Austrian high culture was primarily metropolitan, or rather Vienna-oriented. Then in 1920 came the founding by Max Reinhardt of the Salzburg Festival which was subsequently transformed under von Karajan into an obligatory event for the glitterati.

Today there are cultural offerings nationwide, from gnat-infested open-air operettas at tiny Mörbisch on the Neusiedler See in the east, to avant-garde arts festivals at Graz in the south and at Bregenz in the west. But when Austrian cultural achievements are considered, it is Vienna that springs to mind, for it is the city of composers – Haydn, Mozart, Beethoven, Schubert, Brahms, Bruckner, Mahler, Schönberg and Strauss; of artists – Klimt and the Vienna Secession; of writers – Raimund, Grillparzer, Nestroy, Kraus; of dramatists – von Hofmannsthal, Schnitzler; of Sigmund Freud; the birthplace of Friedrich von Hayek, Sir Karl Popper and Sir Ernst Gombrich. Many of these are universal geniuses and it can be argued that there is nothing especially or uniquely Austrian about them. Yet the quality and multiplicity of their achievements suggest at the very least that Vienna provided an environment in which creativity flourished: as Kraus sardonically remarked, "The streets of Vienna are surfaced with culture, those of other cities with asphalt".

Since Baroque times theatre and opera have flourished in Vienna, the public's taste for mega-shows being as insatiable as it could be undiscriminating. Maria Theresa decreed that "there must be spectacles" to keep the hoi polloi amused and Adolf Hitler played to a full house when delivering his hour-long rant on the Heldenplatz in 1938. (Like many Austrians, he was himself a frustrated artist, the cultural glories of Vienna inspiring in him a mixture of admiration, hatred and envy.) Grillparzer evoked that sense of the frustrated artist which lies just under the skin of many an Austrian and is given expression in everything from to DIY skills to virtuosity on the violin: 'One lives in half-poetry, dangerous to whole art, and is a poet though one never dreamt of rhyme or stanza.'

A feature of the Viennese passion for culture which is replicated on a provincial scale throughout Austria is violent partisanship. Feuding over artistic matters is something that comes as naturally to the Austrians as breathing. Passions of unbelievable ferocity are displayed for and against new opera productions, or for and against a contemporary playwright's latest kick in the national groin. It was ever so: in the 19th century music lovers were divided into a Wagnerian faction, which supported Bruckner, and a traditional faction supporting Brahms. The latter's music has been described as 'exactly suited to Viennese tastes – not too hot and not too cold', making it sound like a lukewarm bath.

But, this is nothing compared to the abuse that the singularly cantankerous Brahms heaped on the mild and inoffensive Bruckner, whose misfortune it was to be adopted as a totem by the Wagnerians. In one memorably splenetic outburst, Brahms dismissed his rival's efforts as 'symphonic boa-constrictors, the amateurish, confused and illogical abortions of a rustic schoolmaster'.

While culture certainly provides an excellent excuse for quarrelling, itself an art form in Austria and one that has been developed to a high degree of sophistication, Austrians do care deeply about music, art and theatre.

An object of veneration is the Vienna Philharmonic, founded in 1842. The orchestra formerly constituted a priestly caste from which women were rigorously excluded. However, arguments such as the one that women "lack a muscle in the upper arm essential to a supreme vibrato" are wearing thin, and the Philharmoniker is slowly being force to change its entrance criteria. Its members (still for the most part native Viennese) receive state-supported salaries of fabulous proportions, further topped up by a steady flow of royalties from best-selling CDs. Subscribers' tickets (theoretically the only ones available) to the Philharmonic's Sunday morning concerts are passed down in families from generation to generation and attendance is a social as well as a musical ritual.

Theatre, too, has been described as 'a necessity of life for the Austrians that takes second place only to eating and drinking'. Indeed it has often been difficult to know where life on the stage ends and life on the street begins.

Couch-potato culture has not yet attained the grim dominance in Austria that it exercises in the Anglophone world. This may be because the high quality of Austrian television acts as a deterrent to mass viewing – although, of course, if they subscribe to cable, Austrians can always tune in to the Friday night soft porn film. Most of Austrian radio is at least twice as intellectually challenging as the equivalent British channel, and classical music broadcasts are something Austrians wake up to, enjoy during their lunch hour and use as the most agreeable of sleeping pills.

Systems

The collapse of empire in 1918, followed by occupation and total war, meant that in 1945 Austria went back to the drawing board. The Marshall Plan, and the achievement of neutral independence with the State Treaty of 1955, released a flood of resources for reconstruction and modernisation. The Austrians had the talent, were given the money, and modern Austria is the result.

The way in which they did it reflects the Austrian genius for mixing the old with the new, as also for aestheticising technology. The latter is, of course, expected to function smoothly and usually does; but it is also required to conform to the ever important national requirement of *Gemütlichkeit*.

State-of-the-art computers are tastefully arranged in restored palaces, as though the original architect had envisaged them there; passengers emerge from an ultra-modern U-Bahn through a whimsical Secessionist pavilion. The marriage of tradition with modernity is a remarkably happy one: the spotless and noiseless metro glides under the ancient inner city of Vienna, sharing its subterranean secrets with Romanesque remains and medieval cellars; trams (relegated to the scrap heap of history by other, less prudent nations) negotiate the streets of Vienna and Graz at an average speed of ten miles and hour, but this is lightning-like progress compared with the daily snarl-ups in London, Paris or Rome.

Austrians are as ambivalent about modernity as they are about everything else, and especially enjoy the verbal demolition of what they take to be *Größenwahn* (megalomania) on the part of architects. Happily for the critics, there has always been a steady supply of projects which combine massive outlay with spectacular uselessness. 'For hare-brained schemes and stupidities,' wrote one commentator, 'there is always plenty of money in Austria. What prestige is there in a project that is merely sensible?'

Meanwhile, the infrastructure is kept going by a continuous flow of investment in public works. The only drawback is that almost every institution, museum, autobahn, etc., appears to be in a more or less permanent state of *Umbau* (rebuilding). Conversations with minor officials, booking clerks and hall porters always seem to be conducted in competition with a pneumatic drill. Notices mushroom bearing legends such as 'Closed on account of building works. We hope you will understand', or 'Transferred to number 14, such and such street, due to renovation works'; or, more ominously, 'Closed for the time being'.

Education

The Austrians have a reverence for *Bildung*, a term that implies the possession of culture as well as mere knowledge. Some of the most brilliant minds of the 20th century were nurtured in the hothouse atmosphere of the Vienna *Gymnasien* (roughly equivalent to the former British grammar schools).

There are nine years of compulsory schooling in Austria and all classes are co-educational. At ten, pupils divide into two streams, one vocationally oriented and one leading to the secondary school diploma known as the *Matura*. Armed with the latter you have the automatic right to be admitted to university. Budget-beleaguered ministers who appear to be contemplating any dilution of the principles of non-payment (university education is free) and unrestricted entry for *Matura* holders are met with fierce resistance from student bodies and other interested parties. Many people privately feel that 'something should be done' about the overcrowding in higher education and the glut of over-qualified people in the jobs market, but nobody can agree on what that something should be.

University has the further attraction that students can postpone their national service or equivalent community service. Since more and more young people are opting for community service, the authorities are casting around in some desperation to make the military service more 'attractive'. (The idea of making army discipline in some way *gemütlich* (cosy) is charmingly Austrian, but seems unlikely to catch on with the officer corps.)

Sport is not prominent on the school curriculum, but an Austrian idiosyncrasy is the week's break at the end of the first week in February, only a month after the return from the Christmas holidays. To outsiders that may look like skiving, to Austrians it's simply skiing.

Environment

Austria is in the forefront of environmental protection by European standards. Indeed, an absurd situation has arisen whereby the European Union wants Austria's standards to be lowered to accommodate businesses in countries which operate under more lax EU rules. This has not gone down well in Austria. People-power has already forced the government to mothball a nuclear power station at astronomic cost and to abandon plans to build a hydro-electric dam on the Danube.

In domestic politics the government has got progressively greener, banning leaded petrol, issuing ordinances for the separation of waste for recycling, and even forcing indignant lighting shops to take back expired fluorescent tubes.

Crime and Punishment

Serious crime is infrequent in Austria and thus, when it does occur, dominates the headlines all the more. The most dramatic recent cases involve apparently reformed murderers (one of whom had been seen on television, discoursing easily and well on penal reform), who seem to have reverted to type after release. These gentlemen successfully bamboozled well-meaning authorities and psychiatrists, a process known as *Schmäh* in Austria.

The undisputed master of *Schmäh* was a criminal named Udo Proksch, who used to entertain politicians of all shades (but primarily Socialists) in a private room of the famous Viennese coffee-house of Demel, which he owned. These contacts stood him in good stead when he became a prime suspect in an insurance scam involving the sinking of a cargo ship with loss of life. After a few years on the run he became homesick for the fleshpots of Vienna and tried to slip back to Austria in disguise. To the embarrassment of certain highly-placed persons, the British authorities at Heathrow were tactless enough to tip off their Austrian counterparts and there was no alternative but to arrest Proksch as he came through immigration. Thus ended a remarkable exercise in slow-motion detection reminiscent of a flight and pursuit nightmare, but one in which it is the pursuer whose legs never seem to carry him forward.

The Proksch affair represented the high point of Socialist-linked corruption that had thrived under the lax rule of Chancellor ('Emperor Bruno') Kreisky. Scandals ranged from abuse of expenses (expenses are a way of life in Austria) to tax evasion and illicit arms deals. One mega-scandal involving massive corruption in the building of a new General Hospital for Vienna has dragged on for more than a decade. Big political names associated with this and other opaque transactions have a Houdini-like propensity for escaping from tight corners. The few who are convicted tend to get off with a fine and a gentle rap over the knuckles, leaving the court with an air of injured innocence, as if the whole thing had been some ghastly misunderstanding.

Austrians are torn between enjoying the show, as yet another affair unravels, and a justified sense of outrage. The great wine scandal of 1985 began as a comedy, when the way in which the perpetrators were discovered became public: the taxman's suspicions had been aroused by the amount of VAT being reclaimed by wine producers on an anti-freeze ingredient (diethylene glycol). The quantities were enough to keep an army of tractors trundling through the winter. Perhaps, pondered the tax officials, the glycol was being used for some other purpose? Yes indeed: judiciously added to 'plonk', it transformed the latter into a much-prized *Spätlese*, worth three times as much. Less amusing was the damage done by this affair to the economy. Exports of wine declined from a value of 440 million *Schillings* to 90 million.

The fact that honest men lost just as much business as the crooks accords with the cynical perception of the man in the street, who always knew that 'the rich help themselves and the poor get hanged for ha'pence'.

Health

The Austrians' interest in health is scientific, or at least pseudo-scientific. Health conversations are sprinkled with impressive terminology, and friendship requires that you listen to a blow-by-blow account of your friends' symptoms, then reciprocate with an exhaustive account of your own.

Diagnosis suits the Austrian temperament, indeed the enormous and well-earned reputation of the Viennese Medical School was founded on it; some 19th century doctors took this to extremes – "I diagnose that you need more diagnosis". A German visitor in 1847 wrote a satirical poem describing learned Viennese professors energetically taking notes as the patient deteriorated before their eyes and finally expired. Death, of course, provided the opportunity for postmortem examination, followed by more diagnostic discussion.

Dietary Health

Austrian males of the new generation are more fitness- and diet-conscious than their forebears. They are therefore less likely to degenerate into incipient heart attacks on two fat legs. The shambling, pot-bellied *Wurstfresser* (sausage gobbler) and the destitute *Biertippler*, who lived from the residue others had left in beer glasses, are dying out, although they always live longer than they or their doctors predict. It has yet to be seen whether the new Austrian with his vegetarian and mineral water tendencies keeps up that regimen beyond the age of 40.

Centres of Health

Austrian medical treatment is provided through a system of mandatory insurance administered by 'Sickness Funds'. These operate out of fabulous glass and marble palaces and their executive layers are packed with the recipients of political patronage. Top management draws the vast salaries customary on such Austrian gravy trains and the government picks up the bill for the funds deficits.

The system actually works reasonably well, probably because most of its funding is direct. Problems only arise when mistakes or scandals occur, at which point, following a well-established ritual, responsibility is passed round the multiplicity of bodies which have a finger in the health system pie: the Hospital Authority, the Provincial Government, the Federal Ministry for Health, the Federal Ministry for Science and Research, etc. Each of these in turn inspects the responsibility with an air of bewilderment and disgust, before announcing that it does not really belong in their sphere of competence, and passing it on.

Government and Bureaucracy

Party Politics

Two main parties bestraddle the Austrian political scene, the Austrian Socialist Party (SPÖ) – known as 'the reds', and the Austrian People's Party (ÖVP – Conservative) – 'the blacks'. They are under heavy fire from the Austrian Freedom Party (FPÖ) who use the colour blue, but whose right-wing faction is referred to (and not flatteringly) as 'brown'. The other two parties represented in Parliament are the Liberal Forum, and the Greens – a fractious lot who devote much of their time and even more of their energies trying to keep their party together. Months of elaborate negotiation usually founder at the last minute in storms of mutual recrimination.

If avoidance of risk is a key element in the national

psyche, avoidance of conflict is the central plank of national (and personal) strategies for survival. A remarkably sophisticated aspect of this is the 'Social Partnership', an unofficial arrangement by which political stability in Austria is ensured by interested parties. Crucial decisions on wages and prices are agreed by a commission which has no legal standing, and are then endorsed by Conservative interests (e.g. the Chambers of Commerce and Agriculture) and their Socialist counterparts (e.g. the Chamber of Labour and the Trades Unions). Deals are struck behind closed doors and then presented to a grateful public via the government publicity machine.

This highly effective system of mutual back-scratching is reinforced by what its detractors call *Parteibuch-politik* ('the politics of the party membership book'). This ensures that jobs in the substantial state sector are handed out on a proportional basis to the People's Party supporters and the Socialist supporters. The system is typically Austrian in that all its advantages can be described as disadvantages, and vice versa. Thus, on the one hand it appears to perpetuate the rigid left-right divide that actually led to Civil War in 1934, and on the other it was devised precisely to avoid it.

Although corruption and the rise of a third party largely excluded from traditional political patronage may eventually spell the end of this type of decision-making, it has proved remarkably resilient. This is because the system is undoubtedly user-friendly, provided that you correctly identify the party with the predominant influence in the area in which you wish to succeed, and act accordingly. No very great issue of principle is involved since the policy differences between the People's Party and the Socialists are now largely ones of emphasis and anyway the parties are in coalition.

Bureaucracy

Austrians are used to being burdened with thousands of petty restrictions, and one of the main preoccupations of any self-respecting citizen is to find ways of evading those he finds uncongenial. To avoid bureaucratic obstructions, *Hintertürln* (back doors) are used, the exploitation of which approaches an art form. However, those responsible for enforcing regulations may also adopt a cavalier attitude towards them depending upon such imponderables as the state of the policeman's digestion and whether or not the dreaded *Föhn* (south wind) is blowing.

The delicately poised ambivalence of the official mind is deftly evoked by Jörge Mauthe in his description of a typical ministry building, characterised by many long corridors. At the end of one of these is a permanently closed door bearing the legend, 'Entry for all persons is strictly forbidden'. 'Since a door by its very nature would seem to embody the idea, indeed predicate the possibility of access,' writes Mauthe, 'to find such an instruction posted on one is more than a little odd. Even odder, however, is the injunction beneath this all-embracing prohibition, namely: Mind the step.'

Austrian bureaucracy is a work of art, and bureaucratic procedure pursues its own remorseless logic to sometimes surreal conclusions. It is not surprising that senior Austrian bureaucrats have often been aesthetes or writers like Stifter or Grillparzer, men who combined absolute loyalty in the sphere of duty with restrained opposition in the sphere of art. Many of them had a creditable record of disinterested administration under the Habsburgs, when the bureaucracy and the army supplied the glue for holding together diverse races and traditions.

Despite this, bureaucracy is something with which the Austrian has a love-hate relationship (actually *Hassliebe* –

the hate comes first in German). One part of him hates its nagging interference in the remotest corners of his affairs, while another part of him longs to enter the halcyon realms of *Verwaltung* (state administration), where you cannot be sacked once you are *pragmatisiert* (on the permanent staff) and days of tenured pen-pushing are rewarded with the inflated pension that such a stressful career naturally commands. In the 19th century bureaucrats retired to the sunny climes of Graz, which was known less than respectfully as Pensionopolis. Nowadays the pensioned official is to be recognised by a permanent tan acquired on several package tours a year.

Individual *Beamten* (officials) can be diligent, charming, courteous and possessed of a high degree of self-irony in the Austrian way. On the other hand a *grantiger* (grumpy) official can be a formidable burden on reason and humanity. It is little consolation to discover that his or her obduracy may simply be due to tactical manoeuvring in some obscure and ever-ongoing departmental squabble, and has little to do with the innocent victim of the resultant fall-out. For example, some six months after a Hungarian was appointed Director of the Austrian Museum of Modern Art, he was startled to receive a communication from the Aliens Bureau instructing him to leave the country 'at once'. Despite his perfectly legal appointment by the Ministry of Science, treasury officials opposed to it had managed to sit on his contract so long that he had technically become an illegal resident.

Less elevated mortals can seek and get redress for bureaucratic blunders through the *Volksanwalt* (People's Lawyer) – an institution whose activities show that constraints on misuse of executive power are taken much more seriously in Austria than elsewhere. The importance of such constraints was underlined by a statement from the head of the Law Society, in which he complained that

Austria is in danger of being 'administered to death', such is the hail of laws, amendments and extensions thereto falling daily upon the heads of the population.

For this, of course, the *Beamten* cannot be held responsible, but it is a situation that naturally gives them a daunting measure of power. A line in the national anthem runs *'vielgeprüftes Österreich'* (much-tried Austria). *Prüfen* also means 'to examine' and the satirists have recast the final two verses: Much-examined Austria (In respect of the Revenue); Much-examined Austria (In respect of the National Audit Office). You may think you will get away with it, but some bureaucrat with *Sitzfleisch* (diligence) in some inconspicuous little office behind a door marked 'Entry Forbidden' is on your trail...

Business

Austria's monopolistic and corporative approaches to business have often been evident, although such attitudes are now increasingly under attack. A turning point for the free market may have been the failure of official chicanery to prevent Niki Lauda from starting an airline. Having triumphed over near-fatal injuries sustained in a car crash, he achieved the considerably more difficult feat of triumphing over entrenched Austrian bureaucracy in his bid to found an airline. Lauda Air subsequently proved to be more commercially successful than the state-run Austrian Airlines the bureaucrats had been trying to protect.

This trend to more competition is gathering momentum; for example, the Association of Opticians is currently engaged in an almost certainly doomed campaign to prevent a chain of electrical stores from selling spectacles at reasonable prices, and even the insurance cartel has been weakened by government action.

Despite, or perhaps because of, restrictive practices, Austria's economy has long been one of the wonders of the post-war world. Growth has been remarkably sustained and the country appeared miraculously immune to the recession which had smitten other countries. This makes the faltering of Austria's economy in the early '90s an unfamiliar experience. More importantly it has highlighted the parlous state of the country's conglomerate state industries, which have finally imploded after years of slack management and (in some cases) corruption. Business and politics in Austria do not always operate in healthy symbiosis. As the state consortia are broken up and offered for privatisation, Austrians hope that such collusion may become less frequent in future.

Throughout the cold war the country benefited from deals with the East Bloc, so that when the Iron Curtain fell, Austrian businessmen had excellent contacts in many former Communist countries and moved in with great skill to exploit the best opportunities. The good news is that trade with Eastern Europe has grown. The bad news is a hæmorrhaging of jobs due to cheap imports from the east (of food, cement, textiles and leather). At the same time, Austrian firms are themselves moving production into areas like the Czech Republic and Hungary, where skilled labour is low-paid and readily available.

Scepticism about business motives in general is deeply ingrained in public attitudes. This is not surprising given the secretive manner in which executives love to operate. When the announcement was made that two of Austria's biggest banks were planning to merge, the puzzled chief executive of one of them complained to reporters that the first he knew about the imminent merger was when the news media reported it.

Conversation and Gestures

Austrians possess such an armoury of subtly insulting verbal weapons that they do not need to wave their arms about to make a point. Indeed, to outward appearances they are a phlegmatic lot. Many a press conference is delivered with a sang-froid bordering on the catatonic; and it is not unusual to see a guest at a party sitting in thoughtful silence throughout the evening, no doubt following the philosopher Wittgenstein's useful precept: 'Whereof one cannot speak, thereof must one be silent.'

The Austrians have an almost infinite capacity for being unimpressed by verbal claims and boasting, the counterpart of being rather easily impressed by spectacles. Frequently heard is the dismissive comment, *Er macht sich wichtig* ('He's trying to make himself important'), and the *Wichtigtuerei* (pomposity) of know-alls meets with a healthy degree of scorn.

If arrogance or deviousness needs to be exposed, local prejudice is often pressed into service. In particular, people in the provinces have a somewhat jaundiced view of the Viennese character which they express in such phrases as: *Du wienerst mich an* – 'You disgust me'; a *wiendiger Typ* – 'a shady character'; or the assertion: *Wer nichts wird, wird Wiener* – 'Anybody who wants to be a nobody becomes a Viennese'. The Viennese reciprocate in kind with slighting references to 'Tyrolean dumplings' or 'East Frisians', the latter a lethal description of people from Burgenland deemed to be somewhat simple.

Grant und Raunzen (grumbling and whingeing) are staples of Austrian, especially Viennese, conversation. "Not to let an Austrian criticize is to castrate him," claims the sex counsellor, Gerti Senger. This is combined, however, with a great deal of personal charm and courtesy, and an outsider might be inclined to think of it as aggression wrapped in obsequiousness. The more refined forms of grumbling are transmuted into philosophical pessimism, the Austrian's talent for which is part and parcel of his faculty for diagnosis.

A vivid description of professional gloom is provided by the futurologist Professor Millendorfer, who once remarked that the outlook for Austria in 20 or 50 years was good, provided that she somehow managed to survive the next five. However, one day he seemed to be looking (for him) remarkably cheerful. Asked why, he explained, "Things are getting better for us." "I am pleased to hear that," replied his interlocutor. "Are the suicide statistics on the decline?" "No," said Professor Millendorfer, "They remain strikingly constant. But everywhere else in the world they are showing a huge rise."

Language

Proverbial sayings in Austria also reflect ambivalent attitudes to history and to national character. Those that have passed into the language typically recall blunders or faux pas, especially of the executive branch. The most famous is *Alles gerettet, Majestät* ('Everyone's safe, your Majesty'), the over-anxious-to-please report of the police chief to Franz-Josef after the Ringtheater had burned down in 1881. (In fact, 386 people were incinerated.)

Many expressions recall the Austrian's dislike of interlopers who tried to impose their outlandish ways on him. *Es kommt mir spanisch vor* – 'It's something peculiar', and the expression 'to make a Spanish face', date from the time when the Austrian Habsburgs imported a gloomy and unpleasant Spanish retinue, which insisted on sterile and rigid etiquette.

There are an abundance of words and phrases designed to bring down the officious or the vain a peg or two; an *Adabei*, for instance, is one who must always be *dabei*, i.e. present, and seen to be present at every function. Similar meanings are attached to *Gschaftlhuber* – 'Chief of the Fire Brigade, President of the Ten-Pin Bowling Club, Treasurer of the Glee Club, Lieutenant in the Salvation Army, all rolled into one'. Officiousness is also castigated in the delectable phrase *Schnittling auf allen Suppen* ('a chive on every soup').

Even *Beamtensprache* (officialese) can be captivating, for who could resist *das lebende Inventar* (livestock) to describe the teaching staff in a school? Or the self-mocking *Löschmeister* (extinguishing master) to describe a Fire Superintendent? Other words derive their effect from their musical or onomatopoeic qualities – it comes as no surprise to learn that *Schnorrer* and *Schmarotzer* both mean 'sponger', while *Kerzlschlucker* (candle-cormorant) is an insufferably pious person who never misses a mass.

In Austria the worn or mundane phrase is always being given a new spin or a subtly-nuanced intonation that makes the apparently innocent lethal, and the lethal sound innocent. In the hands of a master the language is constantly reframed to produce a stream of freshly minted expressions. But an Austrian, being an Austrian, hardly expects his genius in this or any other regard to be recognised as it deserves. He therefore turns even his neglect into an aphorism, like Grillparzer, who grumbled: "You won't get any recognition in this neck of the woods. In Austria they don't hang (the Order of) the Golden Cross on genius; but they'll sure as hell hang a genius on the cross..."

The Author

Louis James has spent ten more or less fruitful years in contemplation of *Homo austriacus*. Despite being in daily contact with the species, he suspects that it is easier to describe the yeti (on which there is no verifiable information), than the Austrian (on which there is far too much, all of it contradictory). Notwithstanding this difficulty he has conducted many hours of diligent field work in cafés, wine-cellars, etc., refining his impressions for the present study, and was gratified to discover that many Austrian friends and acquaintances were prepared to assist selflessly with this.

Since settling in Vienna he has written regular reports on the Central European enigma, chiefly in the hope that sooner or later he will discover a new key to it (the old one having been thrown into the Danube some time ago). If, as seems likely, his efforts in this regard are crowned with failure, he anticipates that few will notice the fact but he will be considerably more popular with those who do.